SECRETS TO CAREER SUCCESS

(Career advice, Job search and interview techniques)

BY NIGEL J ARMITT FCMA, CGMA, AIET

Includes expert advice on job search during Covid_19

CONTENTS

FOREWORD

What is an interview?

As defined in the Oxford English Dictionary, an interview is "an oral examination of an applicant for a job".

This book has been written as a guide and reference book for everyone who needs to attend a job interview. The aim is to provide you, the reader, with a 'one stop' guide rather than having to spend valuable time researching the subject through the internet and various books, when a more efficient use of your time is to research your target career and organisation, and work to ensure you are fully prepared in advance of the all-important interview which could be a stepping stone to your dream job.

Interviews are by their nature a daunting experience for most people because so much depends on the outcome. Nobody wants to be rejected in life, especially as the outcome of a job interview can directly affect the ability to provide for oneself or family. The thought of having to tell family, friends or work colleagues that one has been unsuccessful in a job interview is not the outcome any of us wants. However to receive a – "**Yes you're hired**" telephone call, email or letter definitely is something we all want to share, tell everybody we know and rightly feel very proud of what we have achieved, and excited about where this could lead, both in the shorter term and future career aspirations.

All of the information and tips on how to succeed during the interview process contained in this guide can be put to use to improve performance in every kind of interview situation, whether face-to-face, by telephone or videoconference.

ABOUT THE AUTHOR

A mere glance at the author Nigel J Armitt's own resume quickly demonstrates why he is ideally qualified to advise others on all aspects of making a mark in the world of work, from drafting an eye-catching resume to securing a first-round interview and clinching the role that could put you on the ladder to career success in the field you aspire to.

Nigel has worked for more than 40 years in the UK and globally for many large corporate companies in the private and public sectors, including but not limited to: Virgin Trains, BUPA, First Group plc., Inchcape plc., Barclays Bank, IMI, Lex, Balfour Beatty, BOC, Cussons, Beloit Walmsley, Bolton Gate, Stordata Solution PLC, CIBA Specialty chemicals, HFC bank, Jarvis plc., NHS, The Football Association, Whites Hotel, Claire House Hospice, Highways Agency, Benefits Agency, Bolton Football Club, T&G, Palmcity, Girl Effect, National Citizen Service, Alpha Trains, Cancer Research, Beatson Institute, Amnesty International and many other companies.

During his career he has worked with more than 60 different businesses including start-ups, Small and medium sized (SME's), Venture Capital (VC), Private Equity (PE) backed and large complex international companies and public sector organisations in over 20 different industry sectors. He has been a senior Board director, Non executive director, Deputy CEO, Company Secretary, qualified accountant and Master NLP practitioner.

As well as recruiting staff for those companies from the UK, Europe, Middle East and India, he has successfully run his own company since 1995 and set up a UK subsidiary of European Spanish group which achieved £1m sales in its first year. Having completed a management buy-in, he raised the finance needed to acquire the target company.   To find out more about the author, his profile can be viewed on

Linkedin: https://www.linkedin.com/in/nigel-john-armitt-a7a1144/

COVID-19 IMPACT – ON JOB SEARCH, INTERVIEWS AND ONBOARDING

Job search

Can you afford to put your job search on HOLD now?

This all depends on your current financial situation, if you had recently become unemployed or were already active in the job market pre COVID-19.

If the answer to the question posed is no, then consider that your next job might be short term; something temporary to earn a living to pay bills and provide food, etc.

It does not have to be perfect if it is ONLY for the short term.

Do not become stressed because you are applying for and accepting jobs you would not normally perform. It should not be embarrassing to be working in a role that is different to your career to date.

Ideally, even if different from your usual or preferred career, this short-term employment may enable you to add skills and experience to your resume which are relevant to your future career path, although this might not always be possible due to jobs available in the current climate.

Look in areas where demand for hiring staff is greatest and most urgent, which may give you the edge to be selected.

Improve your skills

It is always good to improve one's qualifications and now is an excellent time to do that.

Compare the skills and qualifications you have with requirements of what you want to do. Decide where there are areas where more qualifications would be useful and make a candidate more marketable and attractive to potential employers.

There are many courses available online (edX classes, Udemy, Academic Earth, Coursera, Khan Academy, Alison, iTunesU, Linkedin Learning, Future Learn, Microsoft training and tutorials) and some are free or can be negotiated at low value.

14 best sites for online courses:

https://www.themuse.com/advice/14-best-sites-for-taking-online-classes-thatll-boost-your-skills-and-get-you-ahead

Class Central has collected a comprehensive list of new courses that course providers have put online in response to the lockdowns or social distancing put in place by many countries due to the COVID-19 pandemic, for free or at a heavily discounted price.

https://www/classcentral.com/report/free-online-learning-cornavirus/

Networking

You should be comfortable networking by telephone and digital conferencing plus through selected social media. Use professional groups on LinkedIn and join virtual events, webinars that will increase learning and promote yourself across your specific industry sector.

There are many sub groups on LinkedIn that will be relevant to your job search.

Keep active on LinkedIn by posting articles demonstrating your experience and asking for comment, which will raise your profile to a wide audience.

You should rehearse a virtual interview with a friend if possible; ask them for feedback so you can improve your style and delivery in answering their questions and learn how to angle your camera to show you in the best possible light. Continue to talk socially to any mentors and professional contacts to practice and improve your confidence in speaking with authority.

Research market intelligence

Check how different organisations are dealing with the crisis and caring for their staff as regards their well-being. Ask yourself - Are they companies you would want to work for in the future?
Are employees allowed to work from home and were any staff made redundant?

A useful tool to set up is Google Alerts which will enable you to receive updates on particular organisations you are keen to follow. At future interviews you will then be able to demonstrate up-to-date knowledge on the company you want to work for. You will be able to show the interviewer how knowledgeable you are and give responses to questions asked which are relevant to the current issues/problems the company is experiencing.

Take time out to think

Spend time thinking through exactly where you would like your career to go in the future, whilst you have time now. The objective should be to achieve clarity on the location, the type of work and the role you want to be hired for. Produce a summary document listing target industries, role types and companies you are particularly interested in. Research who in these companies or connections to target companies you might reach out to and find out if there are any employment opportunities OR who to market your services to. Remember there may not be a vacancy existing today but things can change tomorrow so you should be proactive to make them aware of the skills you can offer them either now or in the future, when they need your particular skills and experience. Remember every interview is as a result of the organisation having a problem/issue it needs to solve. TIP: You must demonstrate why you are the solution they have been searching for.

Maintain contacts in your network

Pick up on previous connections and recruiters, who you have not spoken to for a while.
Send an introductory email to organisations you were previously in touch with, saying:

"I'm looking forward to learning more when it makes sense for your organisation."

This conveys that you know this is an extraordinary time now and also acknowledges that it might not be easy for people to respond immediately.

Ask if there is anything you can do to help them. Mention the skills you have that may be of use to them at this time. Maybe, if you can, say you have experience at leading virtual teams for example. Contact the hiring manager via LinkedIn.

Interviews

Key to success is your remote interviewing skills, which are completely different to those skills required in a face-to-face situation.

TIP: Do not appear "like a rabbit caught in the headlights of a car", showing no emotion or connection with the interviewer as this will result in de-selection.

Pause after each answer you give to questions asked and avoid interrupting the interviewer or talking over them as this is very annoying.

TIP: Don't be afraid to ask the interviewer to repeat the question if you did not hear it all.

Remember to project energy and enthusiasm. Stay focused and carefully answer questions asked. Don't mmm and arrrr when answering questions. Pause before giving an answer it shows calmness and thoughtfulness before you give a considered answer.

Tech tools for hiring such as Zoom, Outlook Teams, Skype and Go-to-Meeting, have been a boon to remote job interviews. Seeing the candidate is so much better than just interviewing them by phone.

Interviews will more than likely focus on your past experience of working from home as it is a different experience from working in an office environment. Potential employers will want to find out about your adaptability and agility in coping in a difficult situation.

Remote interviews are more difficult than face to face and often the interviewers are not trained in how to conduct such interviews. This may put the candidate at a disadvantage but that is why it is so important for interviews to be rehearsed and research completed about the target company.

Beware that sometimes the technology goes wrong and the timing of questions asked and answers given can consequently be out of sync, making the interview experience and selection process much more challenging. Assessments and personality tests are therefore more important in the selection process because of no face-to-face meeting. Hiring for attitude, behavior and cultural fit is just as important as measuring whether the candidate can perform to expectations.

Onboarding

Starting a new job can be challenging during normal conditions, but it can be particularly difficult when you aren't in the office. Proactivity is key If you're onboarding remotely. A good idea is to schedule a lot of brief check-ins with work colleagues to copy the short, informal interactions you'd have had face to face. You should share what tasks you're working on plus asking your colleagues what they do. Understanding the culture is difficult, especially when working from home. Don't be afraid to ask for help when you need it. Focus on all the body language in 'Zoom' meetings plus any other messages including jargon/acronyms used.

TIP: Ask for as much documentation in advance of joining as is allowed so you can study and bring yourself up to speed on the latest developments in the area your new job covers.

Ideally have a 'buddy' or mentor to help you settle in quickly and answer any queries quickly so you are able to be effective as soon as possible. Always make sure you clearly introduce yourself when joining remote meetings. Make notes of key personnel and carry out research in advance, ideally before meetings take place.

TIP: Always find out before each meeting from colleagues if possible WHAT the purpose of the meeting is and the ideal outcomes plus names and responsibilities of all attendees

CHAPTER 1

Accessing the market

The largest professional social networking site, LinkedIn, has more than 675m members (310m active users), 70% outside US, 90m users are senior-level influencers, 63m are in decision-making positions, 92% of B2B marketers include LinkedIn in their digital marketing mix in 200-plus countries worldwide. People are signing up at a rate of approximately two new members a second. It is free to join and post a summary of your career and work history. Recruiters and hiring managers use LinkedIn more than any other website to connect with potential candidates. LinkedIn is more of a professional social networking site than Facebook, which is used primarily to connect to family and friends.

Therefore, for these reasons LinkedIn should be treated in a professional way - and remember - it is a free route to market to advertise yourself on the internet to potential employers, recruiters and HR departments, who regularly use it to find suitable job applicants for free. Researchers at recruitment companies search via LinkedIn using keywords which if not included in your profile will mean you will not be found as a suitable match for particular vacancies they are trying to fill.

TIP: Time spent in writing and perfecting one's profile on LinkedIn is very worthwhile as it may lead to securing your next role. Your profile, just like your resume, needs to be worked on to produce the best possible selling document. It is better to complete your resume first and then 'copy and paste' across to LinkedIn with a few minor amendments. LinkedIn has many advantages over a resume, not least being able to show references from both people you reported to, colleagues and people who you managed in a company. This is essential useful information to any potential employer, as it demonstrates how you were rated and perceived by fellow colleagues.

Articles and videos associated with previous employers may also be posted onto your profile, along with details of any organisations you belong to.

Time should be spent each day accessing certain job sites including LinkedIn to check for suitable jobs.

TIP: Better still sign in to those job sites, which more closely match the type of job you are seeking and input specific job titles, salary range, permanent, part-time or interim, temporary posts and location parameters of where you are prepared to work.

An alert can then be set which will send to your email inbox details of all job vacancies in the future which match the criteria specified, thereby saving you valuable time in searching the internet every day. Then select those emails of only jobs relevant for you to apply to.

TIP: Prepare in advance a cover letter template, which must be customised each time to fit the specific job applied for. This will save valuable time.

TIP: By checking on LinkedIn and on the Internet from time to time you will discover names of new recruiters in your field and you can then introduce yourself speculatively by email to them for future suitable opportunities. Always attach a copy of your resume, latest written references if available and, if you have a full profile on LinkedIn, include the hyperlink in the body of the email.

CHAPTER 2

Top 20 reasons why employers choose candidates

Why do employers select certain candidates?

(What should be demonstrated before and at the interview?)

1. Perfect resume

In the pre-selection process it can simply be that your resume stood out above the competition, 'showcased' your skills and experience plus demonstrated on paper a match against the job requirements of the position. ***The first impression you make is via your resume*** and therefore if this is not the best demonstration of your skills and experience then you will be filtered out in the pre-screening process before you ever reach your first interview. It follows that this document must be updated regularly with your latest experience and skills, as an out-of-date resume will fail you. Check out the competition online in your particular industry to use the best format and narrative, where appropriate, of examples of best resumes. LinkedIn is a good source for checking the wording used in profiles and replicating narrative. Don't be afraid to seek help from resume writing experts or alternatively use people in your network to review your resume for free. There are many ways to check for free with recruitment consultants and other people who are experts in your particular sector. People always like being asked for advice, as they appreciate you personally seeking help from them in your career and it shows how highly you value their experience and suggestions.

2. Personal online brand

Employers will check your online 'personal brand' and therefore it is essential you pay attention to your online profile, as anything, which does not show you in a favourable light, may be used against you in the selection process. Ensure your profile on LinkedIn, if you have one, is also as up to date and matches your resume and does not conflict with anything shown in this document.

LinkedIn is invaluable in that in enables you to promote your unique experience and knowledge by posting comments in groups around subjects raised in your particular area of expertise. Recommendations should be requested on LinkedIn from not only colleagues who you reported to but also others who worked with you plus external parties – suppliers, consultants and professionals

TIP: Ask for references from staff that reported to you (if you managed staff), as this will demonstrate your qualities for managing people and will benefit you when being selected for future managerial roles. Otherwise ask managers and directors whom you worked with in your previous roles. Don't forget voluntary work colleagues.

Remember that besides your LinkedIn profile, all other social networking sites, e.g. Facebook, Twitter and Pinterest may be visible to your prospective employer.

Therefore anything deemed relevant to your application will be taken into account during the selection process - for good or bad.

TIP: Therefore you must amend/remove items on all your social networking sites which you feel may not portray you in the best possible light if viewed by a potential employer or their HR department.

3. Relevant skills and experience

There is no substitute for a candidate possessing the right skills and experience required to perform the role. In today's competitive job market employers can afford to be very selective in choosing the right person, especially when they have received a high volume of applicants. This means interviewees must ensure they communicate and demonstrate that they are fully equipped with the relevant skills and experience. Employers are not going to choose a candidate who will need to be extensively trained, which costs them time and money. Therefore if the target role you are seeking requires additional skills and experience, which you do not currently possess, you should find ways to train yourself through online or classroom courses. Additionally, if possible you may be able to learn the required skills by offering to perform the role for free for a short period or at a reduced rate of pay, whilst acquiring such skills.

4. People person

People skills are key to any role and include being able to work with fellow colleagues inside the business as well as interact with ease with people outside the company.

Not everyone is able to work with different people, some prefer to work in isolation and not be part of a team, and therefore will not be suitable for a managerial or customer-facing role. Success in delivery and achieving objectives in most roles is in direct proportion to how good a person is at interacting and working with other people.

5. Likeability factor

The interviewer will want to feel you have the likeability factor and will integrate into their organisation easily and quickly, and also that your chemistry will fit with those people already in your team so that you are able to work with all employees in the organisation.

6. Delivery of company financial plan

Companies recruit to certain roles to increase income or reduce costs and as a result improve the bottom line by generating more profit, leading to company success. 'Cash is king', which means a company cannot survive by generating a profit alone; a positive cash flow is essential. Therefore recruitment to certain roles in the company structure today is often dependent on the ability of the candidate to be able to maintain and improve cash flow in the business, without which the company would not continue to survive.

7. Positive and 'can-do' attitude

Companies look for people who can demonstrate a positive attitude and 'can-do' mentality. The 'can-do' types of people usually also show enthusiasm in their performance of the job. This type of employee enhances the quality of staff working inside an organisation and results in the company achieving its targets and goals. They are an asset to the company and therefore candidates should be able to communicate these qualities at interview and/or at pre-interview in their covering letter submitted with a resume. Candidates with a passion for a particular type of job will often find it easier answering questions about their particular field and this comes across clearly, leaving a lasting impression on the interviewer.

8. Being a good listener

During the interview it is very easy to not listen at times due to nerves or simply being too keen to communicate and sell oneself to the interviewer. There can be a fear of 'not ticking all the boxes' by not having the time or opportunity to communicate all relevant skills required for the job. The outcome of this happening may be that another candidate is chosen, because you had not demonstrated particular essential skills.

TIP: There is a balance that must be struck in how much time you actually speak at the interview. It is vital to listen very carefully to questions asked and to be as concise as possible with the use of words in an interview, as time is limited.

You cannot plan or assume that the allotted interview time will be extended to allow more time. Due to this limited time constraint communication must be very succinct and if answering interview questions, keep your answers only to the specific questions asked.

DO NOT GO OFF AT A TANGENT (speaking about other subjects not being asked or discussed), as this will waste valuable interview time and not improve your chances of being selected. If more time appears to be available then use it to communicate only relevant facts, which will score you points because they add to the reasons why you should be selected.

9. Loyal, reliable and dedicated

These qualities are essential in any employee and the interviewer will probe with their questioning to satisfy themselves that you have them.

Suggested questions that may be asked below:

"What would your previous employers, staff or colleagues say about you?"

TIP: Your answer needs to demonstrate you were a good employee, or manager if in a management role responsible for staff. Also show how you work with and interact with fellow colleagues in previous companies. Do not be overconfident and show arrogance by saying you can do everything to a high level, unless you can genuinely give examples where you have done so.

"How would you describe the culture, management at ABC Ltd (your previous employer)?"

TIP: Be very careful when giving your answer. Any criticism or faults you talk about should be delivered without any nasty comments as this will alienate you with the interviewer. They will view you as holding a grudge or being disloyal about employers and therefore deselect you.

"What could be improved in the way the company was run or managed?"

TIP: Use caution when responding; do not go 'overboard' and give a long list of faults about how the company is run or managed. It is safer to only give one fault, but be prepared to provide a solution as to how they might improve.

"Describe a previous task or project you were responsible for and explain how you delivered it on time and did you need to work additional hours to deliver?"

TIP: Important to give examples to show flexibility to get the task done through personal dedication – may involve working extra hours. Give examples where you were prepared to go the extra mile.

"How do you think an employer could make staff more loyal and reliable?

TIP: This is a catchall question where the interviewer is looking for you to show them that you do understand what employers should do. The question can only be answered correctly if you yourself do fully understand the meaning of the words 'loyal, reliable and dedicated'

- oyal – loyal to the organisation and prepared to speak up for the company and not 'bad-mouth' them or your employer to anyone, in any circumstances

- eliable – employee shows they are a solid good timekeeper and therefore you show they can rely on you to perform

- edicated – an employee demonstrates they always remain focused on delivering tasks in the job, without being distracted

10. Effective problem solvers

Depending on the particular job and level in the organisational structure, often a requirement for a potential candidate to show they know how to apply problem-solving skills in the role.

TIP: Easily satisfied by giving simple examples from previous roles, where there was a particular problem to solve and how you developed a solution. The problem may have been that a task took too long to complete and there was a more efficient method of completing the task – explain what the new process was?

Explain it and how it reduced the time taken.

11. Longevity with the company

Employers look for new employees who they believe are likely to remain with the company for a long period, which is particularly important because of the high cost of recruitment. Employers do not want to waste their time or money in a failed recruitment process. Choosing the wrong candidate is expensive because it means having to start the recruitment process all over again. Your resume shows how long you spent with each of your previous employers and therefore the question, "Why did you leave?" will be asked. Your answers will determine whether the interviewer is convinced that you are likely to stay with them for a long time.

TIP: Prepare in advance of an interview and write down next to each previous employer a brief answer for why you left. You may have left to gain more experience and develop your career, as there were no opportunities for personal development or promotion.

If you did not get on with your manager for whatever reason, be careful how this is explained, as it may be interpreted by the interviewer that you were at fault and therefore would find it difficult to work for any manager, which may not be true.

An employer would prefer a credible, honest and reasonable answer than what is obviously an unconvincing made-up story, as this will quickly destroy your credibility and result in not being selected for the job.

12. Able to answer behavioral or situational interview questions

This usually means explaining a time of conflict with a co-worker and how it was satisfactorily resolved or it may be about two workers not cooperating with each other.

TIP: It is more than likely this occurred with a previous employer. The key is to explain simply how if it was a conflict the member of staff was spoken to in a calm way and made to understand how it is in the interests of all to work together in a harmonious way. Once the reason for the conflict or non-cooperation was known then a solution should have been capable of being implemented to remedy the situation.

13. Showing passion for the job applied for

During the interview the level of passion, desire and hunger for the job will be being measured by the interviewer. At interview a candidate will need to show just how keen and hungry he or she is for the job. A dispassionate person may be too laid back and not pushing hard enough for a job at interview. The interviewer will then conclude a candidate does not really want the job.

TIP: You must sound convincing and sincere in your interview through not only the use of the appropriate positive words but also body language, which must show a focused and determined individual who wants the job and will not be happy unless they are offered it.

14. Perfect chemistry in the new candidate and therefore able to slot into the organisation seamlessly, without causing any disruption.

Once a new employee has been recruited it is essential that he or she is able to join his/her new employer and quickly settle in to become 'part of the furniture', as if they have always been around and do not upset any colleagues or external third parties. Therefore the chemistry of the individual is the single factor, which will ultimately decide whether the person is a good fit for the job and the new organisation.

TIP: Your chemistry cannot be faked by giving out a different impression of the real you at interview. Most interviewers will see through any disguise and quickly be able to decide if you are a good fit and will get on with your future colleagues and external people who you will come into contact with. Be real and natural, as otherwise the worst result would be to be selected for the job but then in a very short time be dismissed because your chemistry was not right for the recruiting organisation. We are not all suited to working in every type of company because the people and the environment in them may not suit us, leading to stress and unhappiness in the workplace.

15. Highest number of points scored against selected criteria (often this type of selection process is used in public sector or governmental organisations).

TIP: The only course of action with this is to prepare in advance all answers to likely questions that may be asked, paying attention to the listed 'must have' job requirements in the advertisement or job description. Remember to highlight key words and then prepare in bullet-point format how you satisfy each requirement. Give examples from previous employers; the more you list the better.

16. Results of psychometric tests, role-plays and team exercises.

Many employers use psychometric testing to aid them in selection not just in lower level roles but also for management and even senior Board appointments.

TIP: There are many websites on the Internet giving advice and assistance on completing such tests. It is useful to have had practice if possible in answering such tests before actually taking the test for the job, so as to reduce nerves and perform better.

Psychometric test advice websites:

www.wikihow.com/Succeed-at-Psychometric-Tests

www.psychometricinstitute.com.au/Psychometric-Test.../Psychometric-Test-Tips.html%20-

https://psychometric-success.com/expert-help.htm%20-

www.targetjobs.co.uk/careers-advice/psychometric-tests

www.jobtestprep.co.uk/howtopass

Role play and team exercises are used and again it is advisable to research this subject before the interview and if possible rehearse role playing, if you are able to find out in advance this selection tool is to be used.

17. Ability to work well in a team

If the job applied for is part of a team then obviously it is important that you are able to demonstrate you are a team player.

TIP: Give previous examples of where you worked in a team and how you added and contributed to the overall team performance; how you cooperated with and worked together with other team members to produce excellent results and deliver. Show your character in how you interact with colleagues and help the company or organisation to achieve its goals and objectives.

18. Understanding the need for authority and ability to work within your organisational structure – normally applies to non-management roles

Acceptance of authority, being given instructions plus performing tasks at your particular level in the company or organisational staff structure is vital.

TIP: Dependent on what previous roles you have held give clear examples if you are asked of how you performed your job and satisfied your manager. Being able to say you achieved good staff appraisal results would help confirm this.

19. Being fully prepared

Demonstrating knowledge of the employer, products or services, current articles on the Internet, company website or in the press, challenges, finances, history, etc.

TIP: Knowledge should be shown during the main interview session but also at the end when you are asked "What questions do you have for me?"

This is your window of opportunity to use company knowledge to ask the interviewer specific questions about it, using the researched information.

20. Excellent references

Previous employer references are very powerful in influencing the selection process.

TIP: A reference should be as current as possible and relevant to the particular job being applied for; that is it should confirm that you do have the skills and qualities being sought in the new role. A reference which confirms what has been delivered in a job and the before and after situation with improvements is best. The higher the position of the referee in the organisation the better and usually the person to whom you reported on a day-to-day basis. It may also be useful in certain situations to have a reference from a third party provider or investor. Another idea is to show on your LinkedIn profile references from staff if you held a managerial role, as these will demonstrate your management skills.

TIP: For those candidates with little or no previous work experience, give examples of clubs, groups, sporting achievements, as they should be used to demonstrate your skills.

CHAPTER 3

Top 20 reasons why employers reject candidates

1. **Role has been filled by an internal candidate**, which is obviously frustrating for an interviewee because it may feel like the recruitment process was purely to benchmark applicants against the chosen internal candidate.

   TIP: You can ask at interview if there are any internal candidates who have been identified so that you are aware of your competition and will not be surprised later if they are chosen. Also clarify which additional skills or experience they have identified they want the new person to bring to the organisation. These requirements should have already been listed in the job description. By exploring this area at interview, you should be able to demonstrate, assuming you possess such requirements, that by choosing you they will strengthen and improve the quality of their workforce.

2. **Position since removed** from the company organisation chart as it has been decided the post is no longer required and may be merged with another position.

TIP: Always ask at interview if you do not know, why the position has arisen and if a replacement of an employee, ask why that person has left or is leaving.

The response as to why an employee left or is about to leave may give important information as to the real reason the job is being recruited to: It may be that the present incumbent has not performed satisfactorily or there are internal politics with his or her supervisor. The company may be restructuring or implementing a transformation process and this requires a different set of skills in the new person.

TIP: The point is, the more information you ascertain either at interview or in advance by asking your recruiter, the more prepared you will be to ask and answer the right questions so you will demonstrate how you can solve their problems. **This may make the difference between being selected or not.**

3. **Job description (JD) has been changed** because the original brief forgot to include specific skills or experience considered to be essential to perform in the role.

TIP: It is impossible to do anything in advance of the interview to prevent this as it is outside your control. However, it is important to clearly communicate when being interviewed all the skills and experience you possess, just in case the JD is changed and hopefully you are not excluded, because this way you were able to demonstrate at interview you had the added skills and experience anyway.

4. **Similarly not being able to give clear examples in previous roles** to questions designed to prove a match of skills and experience against the job description (JD).

TIP: You must fully prepare prior to an interview, including carefully going through the   job description line by line and writing alongside each of the job requirements, whether skills or experience, and write bullet point reminders of your previous experience. These reminders must prompt you to remember and be able to communicate in concise words how and what was achieved and delivered in your previous roles. Only by doing this preparatory work will you be properly prepared with the answers. It is a good idea to highlight with a marker pen every key word in the JD to ensure you have prepared examples of your skills and experience next to each requirement.

TIP: One way to think about communicating your achievements and skills effectively in the interview is to imagine there are large 'buttons' in front of you, one for each skill requirement. The objective then is to literally 'PRESS' each button to score every time you communicate an example of your achievements, skills against each 'button' or key word. The more times you 'PRESS' the buttons, within reason the more you have succeeded in selling yourself to the interviewer.

5. **Lack of managerial and team building skills**.

    For example, a candidate who said he managed 10 employees failed to respond with clarity to questions such as, "Give me an example of when an employee's performance was unacceptable. What steps did you take to resolve this problem?" It became apparent to the interviewer that although he may have performed a leadership role he was not acting in a managerial position.

    TIP: Only by giving clear examples of managerial and team building experience and achievements with a previous employer can you prevent an interviewer from rejecting you because they believe you lack this experience.

6. **Not demonstrating that you are willing to go the extra mile with a 'can-do' attitude.**

TIP: The interviewer will be convinced if you give clear examples of where you have actually gone that extra mile or shown a 'can-do' mentality, particularly if in difficult circumstances either because of obstacles, people or a political situation.

7. **Employer may feel the applicant is more suitable for another role** within the organisation, because he or she is better matched.

TIP: This comes down to communicating clearly why you are a good match for the particular job being recruited to and if the interviewer is satisfied then he or she is not going to try and match you against another role.

8. **Not being a good listener** because the interviewee tends to speak more than he or she should and does not stop and take time to listen to what is being said or asked of them.

TIP: Concentrate during the interview on the content of what the interviewer is saying. Do not tune yourself out. You have to prevent any outside thoughts from coming into your mind.

Minds can often wander off. Block out any other competing thoughts. By focusing on the present, which is the interview situation, you should be able to prevent any lapse of concentration. Remember, this is your only opportunity of convincing the employer you are the right candidate. You do not get another chance to communicate why to choose you, so concentrate.

Practice role-playing interviewer and interviewee before the interview with a friend or colleague.

9. **More hands-on technical skills required** meaning they need a doer rather than someone managing the work to be delivered. In this situation the interviewer needs to be convinced you are prepared to 'roll up your sleeves' as they believe the task or tasks cannot be delivered unless this happens.

   TIP: If you are a doer then you should say so and that you are prepared to do certain tasks, plus it should be easy to give some examples from previous employers.

10. **Unable to convince you are an effective problem-solver.**

    This may be a difficult situation, matter or person, which led to a problem. You should then give examples of how you approached the problem and what steps were taken to resolve it.

TIP: During pre-interview preparation write down some examples and learn them so they are easy to recall.

11. Not answered satisfactorily a behavioral or situational question.

Question: "A member of your team puts her coat on and threatens to walk out of the office due to stress, so how do you handle the situation?"

Either you have this experience and are able to answer or it is not a set of skills you possess.

TIP: During pre-interview preparation write down some examples and learn them so they are easy to recall.

12. Not coming across as a positive and enthusiastic person.

Employers always seek positive and enthusiastic staff because these types of people make the culture better in an organisation. You can tell within seconds when you visit a company whether it is built on such people from the moment you walk into the reception, speak to the receptionist and talk to its employees.

TIP: You need to project confidence, optimism and focus on good things rather than bad. This shows a passionate interest in your work and achievements to date.

13. **Loyalty, dedication and reliability not demonstrated.**

   TIP: Any adverse comments made about previous employers no matter how small they may appear to be should be avoided. This includes adverse comments made about not agreeing to work extra hours to complete a project on time. Reliability is about being able to be trusted to do what the employer expects you to do.

14. **The interviewer felt the personality was not right and the candidate would not fit** in with the people in the organisation.

   TIP: Knowing whether your personality type will fit in can be explored by researching in advance the type of company or organisation you wish to join. This can be done by visiting their website or social media (Facebook, Twitter, etc.), which will show comments, news stories of employees, company newsletter or other web pages and by searching online for articles. LinkedIn is another source of information as it provides details of any employees who have chosen to post their profile, which you can view. Better still, you might be able to actually speak to someone who is employed by the target employer or has a business relationship, e.g. suppliers or providers, even the security guard at the gate.

15. **Poor preparation** by the interviewee may manifest itself in not being able to demonstrate knowledge about the company or organisation, when speaking about the products or services offered, which suggests lack of commitment and interest on the candidate's part.

TIP: This should not happen to you if you set aside sufficient time to do your research as clearly explained in Chapter 4 on Preparation and Research

16. **Internal company politics.**

Unfortunately, people interfere in the recruitment process in ways they should not. This can be for any number of reasons and it is something, which is outside the control of the candidate, and therefore nothing can be done to prevent this from happening.

17. **Arrive late for the interview.**

Lateness for an interview is not acceptable and sends a clear signal to the recruiter or employer, shows at worst a lack of interest or of planning in advance to ensure they arrived for the interview meeting, telephone call or video-conferencing call on time. Only in extreme circumstances is an interviewer going to tolerate such a lapse in judgement as it shows a lack of respect for people and their time. It also results in most candidates never recovering from during the interview and therefore not presenting themselves in the best possible way because they are not able to keep a clear head. With so many candidates now applying for each job it makes it very easy for an employer or recruiter to reject a candidate because of lateness.

TIP: Prepare beforehand and make sure you have double-checked the route and method of transport being used to take you to the interview venue. Build in sufficient time to allow for delays on public transport. If it is a telephone or video-conference interview, double-check the start time in your own time zone; if the interviewer is not going to interview you in your home country because there will be a time difference between the two of you – **Don't get it wrong and miscalculate the start time!** Arrive earlier and actually walk up to the building and double-check you have arrived at the right venue. It is then hopefully not too late for you to head off to the right location, assuming the distance between the current venue and the correct location is only a few streets away. With satnav apps on mobile phones there is no excuse for not finding and arriving on time at a venue.

18. Not staying focussed on specific job requirements.

People get side-tracked easily in the selection process. This may happen because one candidate has a set of skills not important for the particular job but very useful for another role in the organisation. They may even be attractive as a candidate because of the useful inside current knowledge they bring from a serious competitor. This reason for rejection at interview cannot be avoided as it is the recruiter who is in ultimate control in the selection process but this should rarely happen.

19. Not accepting any responsibility for any previous failed projects, mistakes or poor delivery by teams.

This may be an impression that a candidate leaves the interviewer or recruiter with because of answers to questions asked about previous failures. To avoid this situation from happening make it clear you have always accepted full responsibility if a mistake was made and gone the extra mile to correct it.

TIP: Candidates should think carefully before answering such probing questions and not give the impression that they never make mistakes, but rather they do admit to mistakes and have fixed them or learned from them, to make sure they do not reoccur.

20. **The overall great candidate didn't want the job (or that's the impression given).**

As the selection process uses human interaction it follows it is subjective. Therefore, even though recruiters may follow the same standard process they can arrive at different conclusions about the suitability of a candidate for a job. However, if asked all the recruiters would agree it is not just about the most qualified and experienced applicant. Not being able to convince a recruiter you are interested in the job or failure to show energy and excitement to join the organisation will count above all else and is a reason to de-select a candidate.

TIP: This can be overcome by preparation and research for a job so that you are fully prepared and able to use the time at interview to convince them of your genuine interest in their organisation, products or services offered and your energy and drive to deliver in the new role. Say just how much you want to join them with passion and sincerity.

CHAPTER 4

Preparation and research

It is important to practise answers to likely questions and carry out research online about the company or organisation in advance, though not too far in advance of the day of the interview, otherwise you might forget the facts.

This builds confidence, results in being able to project self-confidence in the interview and helps to reduce interview nerves and stress because you will not be worrying unnecessarily about lack of knowledge or not knowing what answers to give.

To avoid interview nerves and feel you are in control and at ease only comes from thorough preparation, meaning researching and practising several times giving answers to sample interview questions.

Detailed knowledge of the company or organisation, its industry sector, history, organisational structure, product or service sold and current news articles, which can be found either on their own website or the internet is vital. Without this knowledge you are not prepared and should not attempt to present yourself at interview. The more senior the roles in the organisational structure the more data you will be expected to know, which should include financial data. Questions will be asked at interview to verify whether the candidate has done any research. Lack of knowledge about latest developments will always be interpreted as the candidate not being serious about working for the employer. Current events, which have affected the operation of the company or organisation, must be researched and their influence understood because the events may have a direct effect on future profits earned and the job applied for.

Practise answering questions in advance of the interview, bearing in mind what the specific job is you are applying for, as certain questions will be role specific. Remember to fine-tune your responses and continually improve and perfect content and delivery. Use a friend, business colleague or partner to role-play and act as interviewer, as this will greatly improve your confidence. At the same time do not learn the responses like a robot because this will not appear natural and will work against your selection.

You must have studied thoroughly your resume and additionally LinkedIn profile (if any) if it contains additional information as they both specifically relate to the vacancy applied for. At interview you do not have the luxury of being able to reach into your briefcase and refer to your CV to check what was achieved or delivered at Co X; neither can you check when you worked at

Co Y, so this information must be learned and easily recalled at interview.

Your history of previous companies, roles with facts and figures plus what difference you made in each role must 'roll off the tongue' and come naturally, so that you do not become stressed when communicating your message or answering specific questions about a previous role. The interviewer is looking for how you solved problems and what your achievements were, because this is a good measure to demonstrate your skills.

TIP: At the interview, when you have answered the question you should double-check with the interviewer if you have answered their question satisfactorily or whether they would like anything explaining or clarifying further. This is your final opportunity to restate your answer perhaps more clearly and ensure you leave having correctly answered every question to the interviewer's satisfaction and your own.

Relaxing During the Interview

Breathing control is important whilst being interviewed. Remember to take deep breaths before giving answers to a question, as this will calm you by keeping the brain oxygenated plus giving you time to think and organise your thoughts before responding. Your confidence will grow and you will be able to be much more focused and provide a clear concise answer to the interviewer's questions. Keeping your posture in an upright position will aid breathing and present you in a professional manner, as the interview is like a business meeting.

Being genuine and showing a sense of humour rather than being too serious is also important as it will build a rapport with the interviewer. Recognise your nervous habits and practice before the interview, trying to control them naturally so that you do not feel uncomfortable and self-conscious at interview. The more practice you do in advance of the interview the easier it will be on the day.

TIP: Remember you would not be sat at the interview if they did not consider you were good enough to be shortlisted, so you must have impressed them so far with your skills and experience. Therefore sit back and enjoy the meeting and don't think of it as a tortuous experience, in which the interviewer is trying to catch you out asking very difficult questions. If you have prepared well then there should not be any questions you are not capable of answering, providing you breathe deeply and pause before giving a response.

Effective Job Interviewing: 10 Steps to Interview Success

1   Before the job interview, write down several success stories and list key job skills. Write down a few instances where these job skills were successfully employed.

2   Perform some preliminary research on the company and learn about its products and services. Print out several

pages of the company's website and lay them out during the job interview. When asking the employer about the company, make notes in the margins of these printouts.

3   Be clear and concise. When answering questions during the interview, don't ramble on and get off track. Keep answers brief and to the point, yet at the same time conversational.

4   Discuss strengths and job accomplishments. Throughout the job interview, mention your core set of key strengths several times. Include discussion on specific achievements. Be specific, citing three or more major accomplishments.

5   Match job skills and strengths into the company's goals. Talk about how your core set of strengths and job skills match the position and how they would benefit the company.

6   Think like a member of the company's team. When a prospective employee says something like, "As a member of the company's team, you would...," it impresses the employer and displays enthusiasm and proactivity. However do not overdo it and act like you already have the job.

7   Ask the employer questions about the company and the requirements of the position. Towards the end of the job interview, the employer always asks whether you have

any questions. The answer should always be "yes" and you must be prepared with a list of questions to ask.

8   Don't be a one-sided robot. Whilst at all times being brief and concise, the conversation should not be robotic or one-sided. Answer all the employer's questions concisely, but be sure to keep a steady conversational flow going.

9   Pay attention to body language. Do not fidget in the chair. Sit up straight, on the edge of the chair if need be. Do not gaze out of the window or furrow your eyebrows at challenging questions. Maintain good eye contact and smile often.

10 Wear modern clothing and an updated hairstyle. This indicates a youthful appearance. Youth is associated with energy and enthusiasm, which employers are attracted to. This can increase the chances of selection.

Cover letter tips

1   The cover letter is not a copy of the resume

It should be used as your opportunity to make it easy and simple for the reader to select your application as a match against the job description of the role you have applied for.

TIP: You will only succeed by using narrative in your letter which sells you to the reader and leaves no doubt in the reader's mind that you are a good match for the role.

Remember your cover letter is attached to your resume and usually on top so this gives you an ideal opportunity to make it easier for the reviewer of applications to select your application instead of others, but only if it satisfies certain criteria. Your personality and interest in the particular field in which you are applying should come across, so as to show how up to date you are on latest developments, technological and otherwise in the news. Use an Internet search engine, e.g. Google or top20.com (20 top search engines) to research your particular field of work or company/organisation and then use your research findings in your cover letter and where appropriate in your introductory paragraph of why you are applying for the role.

2   Be concise

Everything must be said in one page, therefore use only a few words and keep to the point in describing how you match the job requirements.

TIP: The easier and quicker it is for the reviewer to highlight or tick off your skills and experience against those listed as essential or required for the job, the greater the chance of you passing the test and being shortlisted for interview.

A long-winded cover letter not clearly explaining yourself will eliminate you from the process at the first hurdle.

3   It is best to address the cover letter to the person who is recruiting and usually named in the job advertisement. If you do not know then simply go straight into the body of the cover letter.

TIP: A personally addressed cover letter is more effective because it is addressed to an individual and more than likely the final person selecting the shortlist of candidates to be interviewed, although this task can be delegated to another person, who is given a list of selection criteria to follow.

4   The use of the personal pronouns 'I' and 'my' must be avoided the same as when writing your resume, which should always be in the past tense as it is a record of what you have already achieved, therefore in the past.

5   A copy of the cover letter is best sent as a .pdf document because this will eliminate any problems the recipient may have in opening and reading the attachment. There have been times in the past when recruiters

have been unable to open the attachment due to its file extension. Bear in mind that if this happens to your document the recruiter will often not even respond to you, as they are too busy dealing with all the applications they have received and yours could be rejected because of file type. File extension .docx must be avoided and .doc is preferable, but only where this file type is specified in the job advertisement.

6 Always close the letter with a strong and convincing final paragraph, which leaves the reader with no doubt as to what you will bring to the new role in experience and skills. Keep to no more than two concise sentences, which should leave the reader with a clear impression and make them want to meet you, as they believe you are a very strong candidate and a match for the position.

CHAPTER 5

The Interview

The first seven seconds: One NYU (New York University) research study showed that impressions are made within the ***first seven seconds of meeting.***

This is obviously a very important piece of research, which cannot be ignored by any potential candidate who wants to succeed in interviews.

The employer-employee relationship often starts with the first in-person interview and therefore it is of paramount importance you start this relationship in the right way; alternatively it may start with a telephone or video conference call.

First impressions are of paramount importance and you only have the one opportunity to get it right first time – don't ruin it!

The impression you give is not only what you say to the interviewer but also how you look, including what clothes you are wearing. Therefore smart clothes, which project a business look, are preferable. Casual dress may be acceptable in certain IT and media companies but is not advisable in the majority of interview situations.

An interviewer will always observe your hair and shoes, which project an image of what sort of person you are. Facial expressions can reveal a great deal about a candidate so remember this when you are being interviewed and don't pull funny faces, which may be misconstrued by the interviewer.

An interviewer is more likely to remember you by 'hooks', which may be good or bad, such as the colour and style of your clothing, your hair, unusual interest, sport, team you support, major achievement in your previous career or the way you communicate.

What they remember is down to how you sell yourself at interview.

TIP: **When you arrive at the reception of the venue where you are being interviewed find out where the restroom is so you can check your appearance in the mirror.**

TIP: **Remember that the interview process starts when you enter the premises where the interview is to take place. Therefore you must be polite and present yourself in a business-like manner to everybody you meet at the venue. This may be the security guard, receptionist, other member of staff, and secretary of the person interviewing you.**

The impression left must be positive, as the interviewer will often speak to those same people and ask for their impressions. So arriving late and upsetting the receptionist for keeping you waiting is not generally a good idea.

Remember to always shake the interviewer's hand firmly and look him or her directly in the eye. During the interview do not slouch in the chair but sit up straight, which projects confidence plus poise.

Pause before answering questions as this gives you time to think about what you are going to say and shows that you are comfortable and confident in the interview.

TIP: Using the words 'like' and 'um' is not a good idea as this shows how nervous you are, so practice what you are going to say before the interview, either on your own or ask a partner or trusted friend to play the role of the interviewer which will improve your confidence to present well at the real interview.

You should have rehearsed before the interview by having fully researched the company and made a list of questions you want to ask the interviewer which demonstrate you are serious about the position and more importantly interested about the company itself.

TIP: On the morning of the interview always check the internet for any new article about your potential employer, as this shows you are completely up to date on news and it may be an article about the same area of the business you are applying to work in.

Ideally create an opportunity to mention the news story at an appropriate point in the interview.

TIP: At the end of the interview always remember to smile and thank the interviewer for their time; tell them you enjoyed the meeting and look forward to hearing from them. If they have not told you what the next steps are then do not be afraid to ask, as this shows you are still interested in the role.

An important point to remember is that it is no use charging into the interview trying to show how much you want the position, if you have not first found out by asking more questions about what the role entails. This includes the demands of the job, whether you will be required to travel and if so what percentage of your total time plus the expected hours you are required to work.

CHAPTER 6

Interview Questions and answers

1. **"Tell me about yourself?"**

   Often used as an opening question to start the interview process and 'warm up' the interview. This is an opportunity to really sell yourself to the interviewer at the beginning of the interview.

   TIP: Keep to your professional characteristics, qualifications or training courses, university, college or groups/societies you belong to if you do not possess any qualifications or previous relevant experience. Keep in mind throughout that relevant experience means having a direct connection to the job being interviewed for. Do not waste valuable time speaking about unrelated experience, which is NOT relevant.

2. **"Why did you apply for this job?"**

   The objective of asking this question is to assess how enthusiastic and keen you are to work for the employer and also your answers will reveal if you have done your research on the company and the particular role.

TIP: Only if you have fully researched the company including its culture, vision, history, structure, locations, products or services and understand the job description and requirements can you answer satisfactorily? Your answer should show you match the company's values and objectives and can fit into their organisation.

3. **"What is your greatest weakness?"**

The answer to this question shows whether you are aware of any weaknesses and if so what steps you have taken to eliminate them. Any revealed weaknesses, which will result in poor performance on the job, will not be acceptable to your interviewer.

TIP: Better not to admit to any specific weakness unless you can turn it into a strength by showing how you have overcome it. An acceptable answer is to say you are a perfectionist because attention to detail ensures accuracy. Another answer is you used to be impatient of colleagues in completing a task but have learnt to be more tolerant now. You can also say you are continually improving yourself through training, coaching or mentoring as this will send a positive message.

4. **"How would you describe your management style?"**

Be careful how you respond because you must show you are able to be flexible and not fixed in managing situations and staff. Skilled and experienced managers learn the art of adapting to different situations with a range of styles.

TIP: Give examples of using a different management style in several situations.

5. **Describe how you worked as part of a team?**

Many organisations use teams in their structure, therefore you need to be able to describe a situation in which you worked in a team. It is possible previous roles were not as part of a team. If this is the case give an example from your personal life where you played a team sport or were active in a society or group at school or college/university.

6. **What three things would you do straightaway if you were offered this job?**

TIP: Your answer should include tackling the problems or starting to deliver on the objectives, which have been communicated to you by the interviewer already or perhaps were alluded to in the advertisement. What is important is to demonstrate your prioritisation, organisational, adaptability and learning skills. If a more senior role, then the interviewer will be looking for how you apply strategic thinking to your decisions. To quickly learn about the new organisation, make contact from day one with the key personnel who you need to interact with to be able to execute your job effectively. This communicates a clear message that you know what you are doing and will start to deliver quickly.

7. **What do you know about our company?**

This will quickly assess if you have done your homework and thoroughly researched the company in advance.

TIP: Remember to talk about the values and company vision statement, as this shows you have done your research thoroughly. Products or services offered must be known in detail, as must latest news stories, where they are relevant to the job being applied for, particularly if the company has recently won or bid for a new sales contract. Do not forget to research stakeholders for latest articles and any new legislation which has a direct impact on the way the company conducts its business.

8. **What do you think are the top three things required to be successful in this role?**

Explain how you will quickly settle into the company's culture. You should provide examples of how you did this with previous employers.

Next list which task priorities you would focus on first (as set out in the job advertisement). Finally give an idea of your work style, which may be management style or working as part of a team, with colleagues in the organisation's structure to deliver the task. Recalling previous work examples of similar situations will assist you in answering this question.

9. **What was one of your best achievements at work, which made you feel proud?**

This is your opportunity to show what motivates, drives you and gives you the most job satisfaction at work. It will also let the interviewer know whether you worked in a solo capacity or as part of a team to deliver.

TIP: Remember if the job you applied for requires a team player then it is no use giving an example of a solo performance as this will stand against you.

10. **Give an example of when you took a risk and failed and when you did the same and succeeded. What was the difference?**

Your risk-taking ability and tolerance plus self-awareness, conceptual thinking and honesty are being assessed in this question.

TIP: Be honest and give clear work-related examples demonstrating how you learned from a failure and changed the way you now take risks, by reducing the probability of failure from the risk materialising. If no previous work experience refer to your life experiences.

11. **What do you want to do in your future career and how does this job help you move towards that position?**

Your long-term thinking, personal ambition, development expectations and initiative are being questioned besides how aware you are of yourself to set realistic, achievable career goals.

TIP: Prepare and rehearse your answer to this question in advance and then you will have an appropriate response, which shows you have given the matter some thought. Be realistic and do not set unachievable career goals. Set realistic timeframes also.

12. "How would you react if a team member was not contributing to a project?"

TIP: Key is to have researched the particular job applied for and skills required. Think of a time when you had a similar situation. Next, calmly explain to your interviewer what steps you took to handle the situation and why you did it this way. Diplomatic handling of the team member and keeping them motivated are exactly what needs to be demonstrated.

13. "Imagine you have been given a tight deadline and have just discovered you are running out of time. What actions would you take?"

TIP: This question is all about being realistic on what can be achieved on time and what steps you intend to make to rectify the problem and still hit the deadline.

Suggested steps might be for yourself and/or the team to work overtime, bring in additional resources, assuming available (internal or external) or changing the scope of delivery with the objective of reducing the time required to deliver but not sacrificing the overall deliverables. Remember to include in your answer how you would communicate internally and externally, where applicable to those affected by the delay and what actions you have implemented.

14. "What are your hobbies?"

At first this appears to be a seemingly innocent question. But be aware there is more to this question than initially meets the eye.

TIP: Being overly enthusiastic about the extreme sports you practice can work against your selection for a job because it can leave a lasting impression in the interviewer's mind that you may be likely to have days off sick or injured. Be cautious about your hobbies and play safe with the response you give. Watching sport, arts, charity and voluntary work or reading are all very safe answers.

15. "How would you describe yourself in three adjectives?"

TIP: Without prior preparation this question is very likely to be answered incorrectly.

You must prepare and think of three positive traits about yourself; the more they are diroctly rclatcd to the particulai job applied for the better it will impress your interviewer.

You may want to include good time manager, attention to detail, excellent interpersonal skills, business developer, problem solver, team builder, motivator, positive attitude etc. What you must do is be able to demonstrate each skill with an example from previous roles.

16. **"If I was to ask your previous manager to describe you, what would they say about you?"**

    TIP: Be honest and don't make it up because it is highly likely that your previous manager may receive a telephone call or email to give their response to this question. Your answer should match and not be a lie or an over-exaggeration of your skills but at the same time does not undersell yourself.

17. **One of the most important questions to answer at an interview is: "What are your salary expectations?"**

    A common mistake made by many candidates is to respond by giving a specific figure, when the interviewer has not given you an indication. This response may be given before all the facts about a role are known, which makes it impossible to arrive at a reasonable and fair valuation of what the salary for the role should be.

Once a figure has been given it cannot be taken back and changed. A better way to respond is to put the ball back into the interviewer's court by asking for clarification of the job responsibilities and additional benefits on offer, taking into account the skills and experience you are bringing to the role. Should the interviewer push further for an answer then it is suggested a salary range is given, which leaves room for flexibility from the employer's side and achieves the target salary level you seek.

For salary levels you can use sites such as: http: www.glassdoor.com which also displays jobs available.

18. "What was your salary in your previous role?"

WARNING: Do not give a quick answer to this question, as there may not be a direct correlation between that role and the role being applied for. You need to clarify by asking the interviewer if your previous role and position in the organisation's structure is exactly the same as the job being discussed. If it is not then politely point out there is no direct comparison and you would prefer to give a figure for another more closely related role, provided it is not to your disadvantage. Better still if you can persuade the interviewer to give hints about the salary package on offer.

19. "Would you accept a lower level of pay than your previous job if it meant you securing this role?"

Before reacting negatively to this question make sure you have fully understood everything about the new salary package including all the benefits both financial and non-financial, as there may be free training and career development, time off, etc.

20. **Closing question: Usually "Do you have any questions you would like to ask?"**

This is where your preparation before the interview is important. You should be fully prepared and have in mind a minimum of six different questions.

TIP: It is advisable for one or two of your questions to be specifically about the job itself or the performance of tasks in the role. Another question or two should be about the company or organisation or about some recent news article preferably relevant to the job.

One question might be to ask for clarification on the salary package and benefits if they have not been explained previously, unless the interview was an initial screening interview and not the final interview, in which case this question should NOT be asked.

You may ask "What are the future opportunities for me presuming I am employed?" Add questions to your list if during the interview something is said which you require further clarification on and you were not given the opportunity at the time to ask a question of the interviewer. An obvious question to ask if not already answered is "What are the next steps in the interview process or when will I hear if I have been successful?" which shows you are still interested in the role.

It is advisable to have more rather than fewer questions ready, which should be written down and taken into the interview to refer to.

CHAPTER 7

One question candidates often ask is:

How can I assess how well an interview has gone?

An indication may be the actual length of the interview versus the allotted time given, the interpretation being that an interview, which ran over the allotted time, must have gone well. This is not necessarily correct, as the candidate may have answered questions giving long explanations that were not focussed and did not answer the question. What is important is to come out of the interview feeling questions were answered with clear, concise responses.

Every employer appreciates a brief follow-up message whether by email or letter.

If nothing else, saying that you enjoyed meeting them and would be happy to answer any further questions they might have is advisable as it keeps you in their mind and shows normal business etiquette. If you are given the opportunity to respond with more information, clarification or an example of something you delivered or implemented in a previous role or about a topic raised at the interview then do make sure you respond.

How to choose an interview and career coach?

Every company believes in choosing the best candidate so that its performance can improve. As a candidate, you may be required to go through a series of interviews which would make the interviewers decide whether you are fit for their company or not.

Adequate preparation is absolutely necessary if you plan to pass the interview sessions and intelligent candidates get hold of interview coaches for this purpose. You should expect a professional interview coach to provide assistance in the following areas:

- **Providing tips to reduce nervousness and interview stress**

  When a candidate is under stress, his or her chances of getting selected reduce. Professional interviewers analyse the psychological state of each incumbent. Shivering hands and unfocused eyes give the intimation that you lack confidence. It is a fact that the corporate world in particular is quite hostile and only confident people really survivo.

- **Targeting specific questions**

Interviewers do ask specific questions according to the open position and needed academic qualifications. Most of these questions are asked to get a clear feel for your knowledge level, skill set and behavioral characteristics. A professional interview coach is expected to help you in tackling these questions tactfully and with confidence.

- **Updating the Resume**

Most candidates simply do not have any idea of what needs to be included in the resume even after they have worked for a long time. Even if an interviewer or a panel has to conduct only one interview throughout the day, he or she would simply not have the time to go through multiple pages. An experienced interview coach would help you in modifying your resume so that it has a highly professional look. They would help you in filtering out the information that can be discarded and including only what helps sell you as the right candidate to be selected.

CHAPTER 8

CAREER ACTION PLAN

Your career lasts many years and you're likely to want different things from it at different times. Whatever stage you are at, if you want to accelerate/progress your career and make positive changes, then it will take time, energy and commitment over and above working hard in your day job. Systematic and sustained effort will be needed to achieve that promotion, new role or change in career direction. It is all too easy to become distracted with your day-to-day job and everyday life and start to lose focus. This is WHY you need a written action plan to work to and help you make the changes required.

STEP 1: Write down your career goals, making them tangible and clear;

STEP 2: A plan of action helps break down what can seem a major long-term career management project into smaller bite size manageable tasks. This makes for a more realistic, manageable plan and allows progress to be reviewed against set milestones.

HOW to write a career plan? Simply follow the steps below and use the template provided to create a career action plan to help you keep on track with your career goals.

1. **Firstly write down your career goals.** These may be both short-term goals and longer-term aspirations but make these career goals as clear and specific as possible, e.g. not "I want to use financial skills" but more "I want to move into a finance analyst role within an international organisation using innovative and AI technologies". Your goals must be worded so they genuinely motivate you as well as being realistic.

   What can you do which will help you to achieve your goals?

   - Make changes in your current role – e.g. talking to your boss about giving you additional responsibility or solving organisational problems

   - Focus on the external job market, e.g. updating your CV and LinkedIn profile

   - Set personal goals such as finishing work on time to leave the workplace early to improve work/life balance

   - Set developmental goals, e.g. acquiring technical knowledge you need to improve your employability, developing your professional, leadership or assertiveness skills

- Improve skills or experience gaps - attending online/classroom courses, undertaking voluntary work, a secondment or even work shadowing.

Remember to break down each activity into its smallest components and ask someone you trust to give you feedback on your CV and only upload it to recruitment sites when you are satisfied it is the best document to SELL YOU.

2. Scheduling

You should by now have a list of tasks, which are organised. Prioritise and decide which tasks to do first and in what order. Set realistic target dates for each step to be completed and always put a reminder in your diary as a prompt. That way it keeps you on track and ensures you do move forward. Some activities may need to be repeated. An ongoing activity is networking. Set yourself targets for these too, e.g. commit to meetings at a certain frequency – weekly /monthly? There may be a professional sector/industry specific networking event or local regional event.

3. Help and Blockages

It is a good idea to identify any blocks you think might get in the way of you achieving your goals. This could include lack of promotion in your current firm or not finding the time to attend an online course. Think what the advantages would be by attending and then block out time in your diary to allow attendance. Don't accept the blockage is there to stay – all blockages can be removed – do NOT let anything stand in your way – you will regret not taking action in the future and will only be negative as a result.

Maybe ask your organisation to support your training plans; working with a career coach, arranging mock interview practice, finding a mentor or activities to build up your self-confidence. Never give up on self-improvement; you will feel more empowered and positive with each step you take to better yourself and your future.

Don't be afraid of reviewing and changing your career plan in light of new opportunities or changes in personal circumstances.

It's a good idea to have regular check-in times, after the first week, then monthly, and then at three months and six months to check you are on track. Always input into your calendar so it flags up as a reminder. Along with the review, celebrate your successes and achievements by looking at the tasks you have undertaken as well as any results you have started to see.

Each journey begins with taking the first few steps and then it gets easier as you continue with your plan because it becomes a routine and normal, as though you have always done this.

Career Plan

Form below to capture your career action plan information and keep it easily accessible, e.g. on your laptop /desk with the dates in your online diary system.

MY CAREER ACTION PLAN

1. My short/long-term career goal is…………………………..

2. I will achieve it by …………………………………………
(*insert target date*)

3. BELOW are actions to HELP me achieve my goals faster!

Action (e.g. attend assertiveness course)	Target date to COMPLETE

<table>
<tr><td></td><td></td></tr>
</table>

4. Help and Blockages

What might get in my way?	What will help/assist me?

5. **I will review this plan on (INSERT DATES)/weekly, monthly – give specific dates**

To help you in developing a successful career path.

Visit http://interviews.coach

- LinkedIn (https://uk.linkedin.com/in/nigel-john-armitt-a7a1144)

Career coaching recommendations:

BM: Business Operations Manager, San Francisco Bay area

"Nigel gets my highest recommendation as an "executive career coach and mentor". His unique ability to recognize, understand and explain complex (business and personal) challenges has revolutionized my thinking, and most importantly, my actions. He helped me think, explore and focus more clearly about my future career options and make the right choice in deciding what to do next in my career".

SN Ernst & Young, India

"Nigel was prompt in reaching out and had a comprehensive conversation regarding my concerns. He was a patient listener and gave solid inputs that gave new direction".

CHAPTER 9

MORE JOB SEARCH TIPS AND SELF HELP

Widen your job search

Job advertisements will be advertised on company websites and the usual job portals such as LinkedIn, Glassdoor, Indeed, Monster etc. as well as the specialist sites for your own industry.

Do not forget to also use recruitment agencies and Executive Search agencies too as they may have access to exclusive opportunities not publicly available or offer special insight and be able to provide other ideas for your job search.

Government Jobs

- UK Government jobs:
  https://civilservicejobs.service.gov.uk/

- US government jobs: https://www.usajobs.com/

Farming Jobs

- Hobs Labour Solutions:
  http://hopslaboursolutions.com/seasonal-work/

Volunteering Opportunities

If you are struggling to find a job that suits you in the current climate but you still wish to do something worthwhile, you may like to consider doing some volunteering.

- British Red Cross Community Reserve Volunteers:
  https://reserves.redcross.org.uk/

Keeping your skills up to date – Training Courses

There are many universities and training providers currently providing numerous free online training courses.

Harvard University offers free short and longer weekly courses on an array of subjects ranging from Science, Social Sciences, Business, Health, Humanities, Art & Design, Education, to Computer Programming:

https://online-learning.harvard.edu/catalog

Class Central has information on thousands of free online courses from top universities around the world including Ivy League courses such as MIT, Stanford and Harvard.

https://www.classcentral.com/

Professional and careers networking site, **LinkedIn**, offers numerous training courses with its LinkedIn Premium service. LinkedIn offers one-month free access to LinkedIn Premium when you initially sign up: https://www.linkedin.com/

Centre of Excellence is an online learning platform offering events, workshops and award-winning, industry recognised certification through its various e-learning courses. Take advantage of their one free trial online course: www.centreofexcellence.com

Eventbrite, which normally advertises live events and experiences, is now offering webinars, online courses and virtual conferences: https://www.eventbrite.co.uk/

Findcourses.co.uk is a course-specific search engine for courses ranging from vocational courses to evening fitness classes: https://www.findcourses.co.uk/

It's Who you Know - Networking

It is understood that 80% of new jobs come from networking. You may find that in the current working-from-home environment, your network has more time on their hands, so take advantage of this chance catch up with old colleagues or further expand your network.

Getting Skilled up on Technology needed for Working from Home

With many interview and work meetings now having to take place in an online setting, make sure that you are up to date with the latest technology.

Some popular applications used for video conferencing:

- Skype for Business: https://www.skype.com/en/business/
- GoToMeeting: www.gotomeeting.com
- Teams: https://products.office.com/en-gb/microsoft-teams/group-chat-software
- Zoom: Zoom offers free video calling for up to 40-minutes for 3+ people calls but you can upgrade for better packages: https://zoom.us/

Social Networking

Staying in contact with friends and family is especially important when working from home.

Most popular social networking sites:

- Facebook: www.facebook.com

- Instagram: www.instagram.com
- WhatsApp: www.whatsapp.com
- HouseParty: www.houseparty.com

Maintaining Balance: Yoga & Fitness at Home

Whilst job hunting you need to keep a balance between applications, keeping your skills up to date and staying fit and healthy. Yoga and home fitness are seemingly having a comeback now that we are all forced to stay inside. Here are just a few top picks from the thousands out there.

1. Yoga with Adriene

Adriene Mishler (and her dog Benji) are currently an online sensation having amassed more than a million followers since she launched her YouTube channel three years ago. We particularly recommend her free '30-day Yoga at Home' series which teaches all the basic of vinyasa yoga.

https://www.youtube.com/user/yogawithadriene/videos

2. Yoga Journal

Yoga Journal is a YouTube channel that has many highly experienced yoga teachers with yoga at home classes.

https://www.youtube.com/user/YogaJournal

3. Do Yoga with Me

Do Yoga With Me with a variety of top-notch instructors offers wonderful yoga and meditation classes, all set in beautiful outdoor locations, mostly in British Columbia, Canada.

https://www.doyogawithme.com/yoga_classes

4. Cole Chance Yoga

Recommended by Guardian,offers simple routines and advice on form and yoga.

https://www.youtube.com/channel/UCao6WJ3ryV6IjLmZa-PCv8w/videos

5. CrossFit.com

CrossFit typical involves weights and equipment not suitable for small spaces, but fortnightly CrossFit.com now offers entry-level home alternatives.

http://crossfit.com/

6. Fitness Blender

Husband and wife duo Daniel and Kelli established Fitness Blender which offers a huge selection of videos for home exercise without equipment including fat-burning workouts, kickboxing, strength training, stretches, exercises, etc.

https://www.fitnessblender.com/videos

7. Tone It up: Tone It Up is tailored for women aimed at losing weight and transforming their bodies through simple stretching exercises and offers workouts for specific areas of the body.

http://toneitup.com/fitness/

8. Sweaty Betty

Sweaty Betty offers online classes including yoga workouts and HIIT routines, all levels

http://www.sweatybetty.com/us/free-online-workout-videos/

9. Turbulence Training

Craig Ballantyne is the mastermind of Turbulence Training which provides a collection of workouts and short videos (many under 10 minutes) to help you burn fat and tone up

http://www.turbulencetraining.com/

10. Make Your Body Work

All workouts in Make Your Body Work challenge your entire body and include elements of cardio, strength and core conditioning but with four 'difficulty levels'.

https://makeyourbodywork.com/best-online-workout-videos/

Visit the Author's Website for more information PLUS Career and interview coaching

http://interviews.coach/

GLOBAL JOBSITES

Listed in alphabetical order by geographical region AND More:

Africa

http://www.worldjobsites.org/jobs/Employment_in_Africa/index.html

https://www.careersinafrica.com/

http://www.bestjobsafrica.com/

http://www.arabiahotjobs.com/

Online job portal and recruiting services in North Africa

https://www.devex.com/jobs/

Access NGO jobs

http://www.urgenceafrique.org/

Humanitarian missions in West Africa: Benin, Burkina Faso

https://missiondirect.org/

Charity work. Short- and long-term mission projects.

South Africa

http://www.jobs.co.za/

https://www.jobmasters.co.za/

https://www.bestjobs.co.za/

The Americas

USA

Lists over 100 jobsites

http://www.worldjobsites.org/jobs/Jobs_in_United_States_of_America/

http://www.jobs.net/

https://www.monster.com/

https://www.careerbuilder.com/

https://www.indeed.com/

https://www.glassdoor.com/

https://www.theladders.com/

https://www.job.com/

https://www.snagajob.com/

https://www.simplyhired.com/

http://beyondjobs.com/

http://www.topusajobs.com/

https://www.usajobs.com/

US Government Jobs

https://www.dice.com/

Technology Professionals

https://www.ziprecruiter.com/

Many jobs and can post jobs to 40 job boards

http://www.findtherightjob.com/

https://www.careerjet.com/

https://justjobs.com/

https://www.jobs2careers.com/

https://www.careerjet.com/

https://www.careerbliss.com/

South America

http://www.worldjobsites.org/jobs/Employment_in_Central_and_South_America/

Jobs, careers, employment opportunities in Central and South America including Caribbean

https://www.latintopjobs.com/

Asia

https://matadornetwork.com/

http://www.worldjobsites.org/jobs/Employment_in_Asia/index.html

https://www.jobstreet.com/

China

http://www.worldjobsites.org/jobs/Jobs_in_China/index.html

http://www.chinajob.com/

https://www.chinajobs77.com/

https://www.jobboardfinder.com/news/the-most-influential-job-boards-in-china/

https://www.jobsitechina.com/12-most-popular-job-websites-in-China.htm

https://www.foreignhr.com/

https://www.cjol.com/

https://www.chinawhisper.com/top-10-best-job-search-websites-in-china/

Overview of all job boards

https://www.zhaopin.com/

Based in Beijing (in Chinese)

httpc://www.toacherhorizons.com/

https://teachinternational.edu.au/teach-abroad-programs/

Teaching jobs - China

https://www.asiaemployment.com.sg/

Jobs in Asia and Middle East

https://www.techinasia.com/jobs

https://www.51job.com/

Publicly owned with twenty-five city offices in mainland China and Hong Kong. Offers a wealth of services to both job seekers and employers in the fields of recruitment, training, assessment and human resources-related areas.

https://www.jobsdb.com/

JobsDB, founded in 1998, is a regional online recruitment centre in the Asia Pacific, which is very popular in China.

https://www.monster.com.hk/

Monster.com, one of the top ten job websites worldwide that was founded in 1994, has a huge presence also in China, especially in Hong Kong.

http://www.12333.gov.cn/

Shanghai Municipal Labour and Social Security Bureau is one of the government agencies within the government control, which aims to increase the strength of its labourers within the country.

http://www.wang-li.com

Wang and Li Company is a major human resources services provider, which has a specialty of managing highly skilled professionals in

Greater China since 1994. Company provides through its website are resume submission, job search and forums.

http://www.chinajob.com/

For Science and Technology or Education. ChinaJob is managed by the China Association for International Exchange of Personnel and China Services International.

https://www.siphrd.com/html/

Suzhou Industrial Park Human Resources Development is connected to the Organization and Personnel Bureau of Suzhou Industrial Park Administrative Committee, has grown quite a lot since May 1995. Career advice and help for recently graduated students.

https://beijing.ixpat.com/

Forum and jobs section especially for expatriates. No agency fees are paid.

http://chinahot.com/

English language job board for expats and foreigners

https://www.echinacities.com/

https://china.xpatjobs.com/

Hong Kong

https://www.reed.co.uk/jobs/hong-kong-jobs

https://www.monster.com.hk/

Japan

https://www.jobsinjapan.com/

New online guide with information on finding work and getting settled in.

https://gaijinpot.com/

Find jobs, apartments, news, classifieds and your guide to business and living in Japan at GaijinPot, the biggest community site for all things Japan.

https://www.jobstreet.com.ph/en/job-search/japan-jobs/

Search thousands of Jobs in at JobStreet.com. Find new employment in, Tokyo, Kobe and Asia. Employers, advertise jobs and find resumes here.

https://www.tofugu.com/jobs/

Hopefully they can offer some insight regarding what you'd be getting yourself into if you decide to live and work in Japan.

https://www.ohayosensei.com/

O-Hayo Sensei, a free, twice-monthly newsletter, is the world's oldest and largest jobs-in-japan publication. Each issue of O-Hayo Sensei researches and lists

https://www.japanenglishteacher.com/

Find English teaching **jobs in Japan**. Japan's No.1 English teaching job site

http://myshigoto.com/

Find jobs in Japan for English speakers or Japanese speakers, teaching jobs as well as non-teaching, in Tokyo and elsewhere in Japan.

Malaysia

https://www.jobstreet.com.my/

Singapore

https://sg.jobsdb.com/

https://sg.jobrapido.com/?q=singapore

Lists all jobs in Singapore

India

http://www.worldjobsites.org/jobs/Jobs_in_India/

https://www.naukri.com/

http://www.jobsahead.com/

https://www.monsterindia.com/

https://www.placementindia.com/

https://www.naukri2000.com/

http://www.jobsbazaar.com/

https://www.careerindia.com/

http://www.india-2000.itgo.com/

http://www.bharatcareers.com/

http://www.careerage.com/

https://www.allindiajobs.in/

https://www.careerindia.com/

https://www.indianjobsite.com/

https://www.freshersworld.com/

https://careergraph.com/

http://www.careermosaicindia.com/

https://www.dice.com/

http://www.jobs-bank.com/

http://www.alltimejobs.com/

Australasia

Australia

http://www.worldjobsites.org/jobs/Jobs_in_Australia/

https://www.careerone.com.au/

https://www.job.com.au/

https://www.seek.com.au/

https://www.australia-mining.com/

Mining jobs

New Zealand

https://www.nzherald.co.nz/tags/employment/11/

https://www.seek.co.nz/

https://www.trademe.co.nz/jobs

http://search4jobs.co.nz/

https://www.job.co.nz/

https://www.job.co.nz/

Europe

https://www.eurojobs.com/

Europe's largest multi-country jobsite for international job opportunities.

https://www.eurojobsites.com/

http://jobs.euractiv.com/

https://www.europeanjobdays.eu/en

Leader in jobs in Brussels and EU affairs.

https://www.eurojobsites.com/

EU Affairs dedicated Job board - EU Jobs in Brussels

UK

http://www.worldjobsites.org/jobs/Jobs_in_United_Kingdom/

http://urlm.co.uk/www.alljobsuk.com

https://www.jobsite.co.uk/

https://www.totaljobs.com/

Total Jobs is another good one with thousands of jobs and good search facilities

https://www.jobs.nhs.uk/

NHS Jobs is the first place to go for NHS jobs, you can save, manage and view your applications online

http://jobs.guardian.co.uk/

Jobs advertised by one the best of the national newspapers, The Guardian

https://www.tes.com/jobs/

The TES community, good for education jobs

https://jobseekers.direct.gov.uk/

Directgov - official job centre website, user-friendly with good search options including filters for date added, PT/FT, temporary / permanent

https://www.reed.co.uk/

Reed - lots of jobs with good search facilities, including location, job type, sector, salary and date job added

https://www.monster.co.uk/

Monster - good search options, can select to only view most recent job posts

https://www.fish4.co.uk/jobs/

Fish4Jobs

https://www.everyjobsite.co.uk/

Everyjobsite - does a good job of collating results from other sites in an easy to use format

https://www.jobsite.co.uk/

Jobsite

https://interim-hub.com/

Interim job site – includes full list of all main interim providers and much more interim resources

https://www.exec-appointments.com/

Executive jobs in UK and overseas

Middle East

http://www.worldjobsites.org/jobs/Employment_in_Middle_East_and_the_Gulf_region/

Middle East and Gulf countries

https://www.bayt.com/

https://www.gulftalent.com/

https://www.arabianbusiness.com/jobs

https://waytogulf.com/jobs/myjobs/

https://www.monstergulf.com/

http://www.gulfjobsmarket.com/

http://www.arabiahotjobs.com/

Online job portal and recruiting services in Middle East and North Africa

http://www.careermideast.com/

Online recruitment and career development services for employers and job seekers

https://gulfbankers.com/

Banking opportunities

https://jobsataramco.eu/

Jobs at Saudi Aramco

Russia

https://russia.xpatjobs.com/

Expat jobs

https://www.gojobs.ru/

Executive level positions

Keeping motivated during a Job Search

https://www.monster.co.uk/career-advice/planning-a-job-search/looking-for-a-job

Conducting a *job search* can put you through a wide variety of emotions until you get the result you're looking *for*.

https://www.careerthinker.com/keeping-motivated/

Tips of Methods *for Staying Motivated During* your Career *Job Search* while ... What we do *for* a living to support ourselves and our families is a huge *part* of ...

https://money.usnews.com/money/blogs/outside-voices-careers/2010/10/19/20-ways-to-stay-motivated-during-your-job-search

20 Ways to *Stay Motivated During* Your *Job Search* ... What all this means is that a major *part* of anyone's *job* hunt is *staying motivated*. We all ...

https://www.forbes.com/sites/jacquelynsmith/2013/01/30/30-motivational-quotes-for-job-seekers/

Are you a tired and frustrated *job* seeker who could use little encouragement? Here are 30 motivational quotes that may help.

https://graduatefog.co.uk/advice/stay-motivated/

Graduate Fog knows that the hardest *part* of *job* hunting has nothing to do with perfecting your CV or preparing *for* interviews. It's finding the will to *keep* going on

Positive Thinking

https://www.freeaffirmations.org/positive-thinking-positive-affirmations

Increase **positive thinking** naturally with these free **affirmations** - Overcome deeply ingrained negativity, change old beliefs, and live a happier life!

http://www.vitalaffirmations.com/

Develop a powerful positive mindset. Learn how to use Affirmations and Positive thinking to manifest positive life changes. Try our free affirmation cards!

https://www.actionforhappiness.org/

Stop getting stuck in negative **thinking** patterns

https://uk.tm.org/

Official Transcendental Meditation organisation in UK

https://tinybuddha.com/blog/10-tips-to-overcome-negative-thoughts-positive-thinking-made-easy/

Negative thoughts drain your energy. The more you give in to them, the stronger they become. Here are a few tips to turn your negative thoughts *positive*.

Stress Management

https://www.wellbeing.work/

Courses and advice, work related

https://www.mayoclinic.org/healthy-lifestyle/stress-management/basics/stress-basics/

Stress management: Learn why you feel stress and how to fight it

https://www.verywellmind.com/stress-management-4157211

https://www.medicinenet.com/search/mni/stress%20management

Learn ways to manage stress with reduction techniques, *exercises*, *stress- management* strategies and meditation

https://www.innerhealthstudio.com/stress-management-exercises

Are you feeling stressed? These stress management exercises include relaxation techniques, time management, and other effective ways to deal with stress.

https://www.mindtools.com/search?search_term=Managing+Stress
Affirmations are positive, specific statements that help you to overcome self- sabotaging, negative thoughts. They help you visualize, and believe in, what you' re ...

Networking (by Continent)

Africa

https://www.the-network.com/member-job-boards/africa/

South Africa

https://www.networkrecruitment.co.za/

The Americas

USA

https://money.usnews.com/money/blogs/outside-voices-careers/2012/04/24/8-handy-sites-for-finding-networking-events

When **career** experts talk about **job** searching, the term "**networking**" is ...

The following sites host professional **events** all over the **United States**:

https://www.thefeng.org/

The FENG is not just another "social **networking**" site or a **job** board. ... We have chapters in almost all the major cities in the **U.S.** as well as many other countries **India**

https://www.indianangelnetwork.com/

India's Largest Angel Network. Indian Angel Network is India's first & largest business angel group with successful entrepreneurs and dynamic CEOs

https://www.meetup.com/topics/job-search/

https://www.meetup.com/topics/networking-for-job-seekers/

Helps groups of people with shared interests plan meetings and form offline clubs ... As an estimated 60% of job offers come from networking,

South America

https://www.ses.com/networks-latin-america

Asia

https://www.the-network.com/member-job-boards/asia/

China

http://www.chopsticksclub.com/

China-UK knowledge sharing, cultural & business exchange, jobs and networking

https://www.linkedin.com/company/cbsn-chinese-business-social-network

https://www.meetup.com/cbsnuk/

https://www.eventbrite.com/d/china--beijing/networking/

https://www.dragonsocial.net/blog/social-media-in-china/

https://www.amchamchina.org/events/

We organize regular networking events, including monthly chapter mixers, consulate briefings, and informative seminars

Hong Kong

https://geoexpat.com/resources/social-networking/

https://www.meetup.com/cities/hk/

https://hkas.uk/

India

https://www.indianangelnetwork.com/

India's Largest Angel Network. Indian Angel Network is India's first & largest business angel group with successful entrepreneurs and dynamic CEOs

https://www.indgovtjobs.in/

Indian Government jobs network

https://www.meetup.com/cities/in/

Japan

https://injapan.gaijinpot.com/category/work/networking-events/

https://jobsinjapan.com/blog/living-in-japan-guide/tokyoexpatnetwork/

Singapore

https://culture360.asef.org/opportunities/job-project-administrator-arts-network-asia-singapore/

The Arts Network Asia (ANA), a regional arts network and regrant group of artists, cultural workers and arts activists from Asia and Singapore

http://www.sandboxadvisors.com/find-jobs-singapore/job-search-networking

https://www.meetup.com/topics/professional-networking/sg/singapore/

Australasia

Australia

https://herbusiness.com/

Women Business Owners Networking

https://www.qld.gov.au/jobs/career/networking/networking

Queensland Government on Networking

New Zealand

https://www.robertwalters.co.nz/career-advice/successful-networking-in-new-zealand.html

https://www.eventbrite.co.nz/d/new-zealand/networking/

https://www.networknz.nz/

Europe

UK

https://www.meetup.com/cities/gb/17/london/career-business/

https://career-advice.jobs.ac.uk/career-development/networking-how-to-maximize-opportunities-and-boost-your-career-connections/

https://www.meetup.com/topics/career-network/

https://www.findnetworkingevents.com/

Search for business networking events, business clubs and networking groups in your local area. Yellow Circle wins UK contract for Business for Breakfast.

https://bni.co.uk/en-GB/index

BNI – The World's Leading Business Networking and Referral Organisation

https://www.4networking.biz/4networkingonline/

UK-wide business networking. With a 4N Passport visit ... I've been to other networking events & always come away feeling that 4N tops them all!

https://www.wibn.co.uk/

The Women in Business Network.tv allows like-minded women to share business for groups in this region, and of course from women elsewhere in the U.K!

https://startups.co.uk/what-business-networking-groups-are-available/

Advice from Start-ups on small business networking groups to help UK entrepreneurs develop client relations to ensure small business success.

https://www.ukbaa.org.uk/member/angelnews/

Looking to join the next big thing? Events in 15 UK cities

https://www.mumandcareer.co.uk/networking-for-women/

Networking for women. in London and Surrey.

https://www.businessbiscotti.co.uk/

Business Biscotti is a dynamic business networking community that powerfully combines local group meetings, with online business networking and real life, fun

https://www.meetup.com/London-European-Club/

London European Club

Middle East

https://careerinyoursuitcase.com/?s=networking

https://www.meed.com/2020-events-set-to-shape-the-middle-east

MEED's comprehensive portfolio covers large-scale summits and conferences to

unique one-to-one networking opportunities and clubs.

https://gbievents.com/

UK. EUROPE. NORTH AMERICA. **MIDDLE EAST**. AFRICA ... Intelligence to our

members and clients. Global Business **Events** - The Heart of your **network** ...

https://www.ibwgabudhabi.org/

International Business Women's Group, Abu Dhabi offers women

opportunities to expand their network

https://www.middleeastinvestmentnetwork.com/

The Middle East Investment Network allows businesses to reach potential angel

investors located around the world. We help build investment partnerships ...

Russia

https://www.eventbrite.com/d/russia--moscow/networking/